AMISTAD

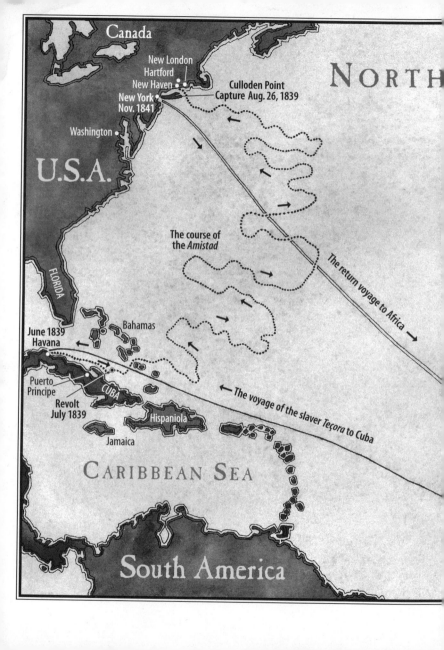

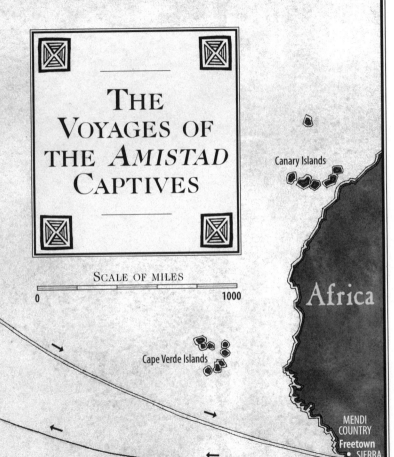

ATLANTIC OCEAN

N

THE
VOYAGES OF
THE *AMISTAD*
CAPTIVES

SCALE OF MILES

0   1000

Canary Islands

Africa

Cape Verde Islands

MENDI
COUNTRY
Freetown
SIERRA
LEONE

Lomboko Harbor
March 1839

AMISTAD

The Slave Uprising Aboard the Spanish Schooner

HELEN KROMER

THE PILGRIM PRESS
CLEVELAND, OHIO

The Pilgrim Press, Cleveland, Ohio 44115

Originally published by Franklin Watts, Inc., as *The Amistad Revolt, 1839: The Slave Uprising Aboard the Spanish Schooner,* © 1973 by Helen Kromer. Preface © 1997 by Helen Kromer.

Artwork: Amistad Research Center, New Orleans, Louisiana: pp. 4, 10, 17, 43, 79, 89; Library of Congress: p. 46; New Haven Colony Historical Society: p. 32; Talladega College, Talladega, Alabama: pp. 20, 21; The Yale University Library: p. 96

02 01 00 99 98 97   5 4 3 2 1

Library of Congress Cataloging-in-Publication Data
Kromer, Helen.
    [Amistad revolt, 1839]
    Amistad : the slave uprising aboard the Spanish schooner /
Helen Kromer.
        p.   cm.
    Originally published: The Amistad revolt, 1839. New York :
F. Watts, 1973.
    ISBN 0-8298-1265-2 (pbk. : alk. paper)
    1. Slavery—United States—Insurrections, etc.   2. Amistad
(Schooner)   I. Title.
E447.K7   1997
326'.0973—dc21
                                            97-44494
                                            CIP

This book is

affectionately dedicated

to my niece,

Elizabeth

CONTENTS

PREFACE

I became fascinated by the epic story of the *Amistad* uprising years ago when I was doing research for a historical filmstrip. The account I read of Africans who rebelled against their captors on the high seas aboard the slave ship *Amistad* in 1839 seized my imagination for many reasons. It was a classic example of the conflict between the highest hopes of our founding fathers for equality and the economic and political sanctioning of slavery. The extraordinary issues raised by the *Amistad* uprising brought together equally uncommon men, from the charismatic African leader Cinque, who was willing to risk death for freedom, to the dedicated abolitionists Lewis and Arthur Tappan, who jeopardized their lives and goods to support emancipation, to the former American president John Quincy Adams, who, though old and tired, gambled his secure reputation to argue the case for the Africans before the Supreme Court.

The *Amistad* uprising was one of those pivotal events that brought the horrors of slavery to the forefront of American consciousness, adding fuel to the abolitionists' fire. When the crippled slave ship was towed into New London, Connecticut, those New Englanders who had turned away from slavery were confronted with incoming slaves. The courts immediately faced the issue whether the Africans on board were people with human rights or property that should be returned to the Spanish owners of the schooner.

The attempt to answer this question resulted in a series of trials that revealed the power of the press and the potency of public recognition that followed. When John Quincy Adams joined the Africans' defense team, he gave their cause enormous authority, which only added to the publicity the newspapers had initiated as soon as the ship had been sighted off the beaches of Long Island.

When I visited libraries to read newspaper accounts of the *Amistad* incident, I learned that the coverage was both constant and compelling. The press reported every aspect of the case, from the incarceration of the Africans to their regular exercise sessions on the New Haven village green outside their jail. Entrepreneurs hawked pictures of the prisoners and sold tickets to an exhibit of masks molded in black wax. The jailer charged a fee so crowds of curiosity seekers could enter the jail and see the prisoners in their cells. The money earned lined the pockets of these enterprising merchants, but it also helped the cause of emancipation. The pervasive attention humanized the captured Africans, transforming them into real people with fears, aspirations, and dignity. Word about the plight of the prisoners spread around the world. Even Queen Victoria spoke up about the case, calling upon the Spanish royal court to free the hapless prisoners and bring the Spanish slavers to trial.

At the time my book about the revolt was first published in 1973, the world seemed to have forgotten about the *Amistad.* Today there is an explosion of interest in this dramatic tale. Autumn of 1997 saw the Chicago Lyric Opera premiere of *Amistad,* directed by George C. Wolfe, composed by Anthony Davis, and with a libretto by Thulani Davis. Steven Spielberg's feature film *Amistad* opened and several television specials went into production. The state of Connecticut commemorated its role as the site of the Africans' imprisonment with the commission of a stunning bronze sculpture depicting Cinque's capture, trial, and return to Africa. The work, mounted in front of New Haven's city hall, is within sight of the famous exercise green. In nearby Mystic Seaport, the keel of a reproduction of the schooner *Amistad* was laid for what will become a floating museum, berthed in Mystic and staffed by inner-city men and women who will sail along both coasts of the nation before circumnavigating the globe.

The sudden attention lavished on this landmark event is astonishing, but it is also shameful and sad that it has taken so long to reach the general public. For the *Amistad* incident was a seminal event that helped shape history. It placed the issue of whether people were property before the Supreme Court of the United States and on the floor of Congress. Following the resolution of the case, members of Congress formed the Select Committee on Slavery, which backed bills and resolutions that opened the discussion among lawmakers, in spite of the slaveholders' angry objections. This kind of increasingly bitter debate came years before the Dred Scott decision, before John Brown's raids, and before the publication of Harriet Beecher Stowe's novel *Uncle Tom's Cabin*—but all of it sailed on the winds of change that began to blow when a group of black Africans rose up to fight for freedom.

Cinque and the *Amistad* ignited the fires that inflamed and illuminated the pro-slavery and anti-slavery forces, pushing the cause of emancipation steadily forward. Out of the committees formed to support the *Amistad* captives grew a new commitment to freeing slaves in the United States. Committees became missions and missions became movements. The most remarkable one, the American Missionary Association, was responsible for developing literally thousands of institutions and programs dedicated to the education of freed blacks. Even as the abolitionists had taught the freed *Amistad* Africans to read and write, so did they organize massively to educate all freed slaves after the Civil War. Wherever arms were laid down, books and chalk were picked up. Five hundred primary and secondary black schools were founded following the Civil War. Ten historically black institutions of higher education remain today. Today's American Missionary Association of the United Church of Christ supports programs of advocacy and empowerment for all peoples.

For the truth is, the schooner *Amistad* left a very long wake behind it. Arriving on these shores at a most propitious time—a time of moral soul-searching, a time of widespread reform—the *Amistad* aroused Americans who were rethinking the meaning of their Declaration of Independence. It was this confluence of place, time, and uncommon people that I found so moving and memorable: that blacks and whites came together for their common good in New England in 1839, a collaboration whose remarkable results are still at work today. *Amistad* will never again be an unknown word.

THE AMISTAD REVOLT

Toward the end of August 1839, ships along the northeastern coast of the United States reported sighting a "suspicious vessel," a "long, low, black schooner," a "sinister ship of indefinite origin," her "sails nearly all blown to pieces and in an almost helpless condition with 25 persons on deck . . . and a large number . . . in a state of starvation—all black men." The mystery ship was the *Amistad,* whose cargo of African slaves had mutinied against the white captain and crew. Between August 26, 1839, when the ship was boarded and the slaves were taken captive, and March 9, 1841, when the slaves were declared freemen by the

Supreme Court of the United States, the mystery of the ship was unraveled before the American public.

Principals

JOHN QUINCY ADAMS, former president of the United States, and in 1839 a member of the House of Representatives, who, as a lawyer, helped to defend the Africans.

ANTONIO, a mulatto cabin boy, slave of the *Amistad*'s captain.

ROGER S. BALDWIN, an antislavery lawyer, who also helped to defend the Africans.

JAMES COVEY, a freed slave serving in the British navy, who acted as interpreter for the Africans.

LIEUTENANT COMMANDER THOMAS R. GEDNEY, commander of the United States surveying brig *Washington.*

JOSIAH GIBBS, professor of Hebrew at Yale College and a specialist in languages.

KA-LI (sometimes spelled Ka-le), TEME, KAGNE (sometimes spelled Kenyee), and MARGRU (sometimes spelled Marngroo), the four African children who were on board the ship.

PEDRO MONTES, an elderly Spaniard, a passenger on the *Amistad,* and the slave purchaser of the four children.

COLONEL AND MRS. PENDLETON, keepers of the tavern-jail in New Haven, Connecticut.

JOSÉ RUIZ, a young Spaniard traveling on the *Amistad* and the slave purchaser of the forty-nine adult Africans.

SINGBE (whose name was sometimes written as Cinque, Cinquez, or Joseph Cinques), a native of Africa sold into slavery, who led the forty-eight other Africans in a revolt aboard the *Amistad*.

LEWIS TAPPAN, a New York merchant and one of the foremost abolitionists of the day.

PRESIDENT MARTIN VAN BUREN, president of the United States.

NOTE: The captives in the account are listed by their African names, though the Spaniards who bought them in Havana gave them Spanish names and the abolitionists in the United States gave them English names.

AMISTAD

WERE THEY PIRATES?

In the autumn of 1839, a small boy named Alonzo Lewis, who lived in Plainville, Connecticut, was standing on the towpath bridge over the canal that ran through his village on its way from New Haven, Connecticut, to Northampton, Massachusetts. Dozens of other people—friends and neighbors—were also crowded along the bridge and the banks of the canal. Years later, he wrote down what he saw:

> Looking northward, I saw a canal-boat approaching. On the upper deck, in two rows facing each other, sat some fifty or more Negroes wrapped in white woolen blankets. . . . To my childish eyes

they presented a truly ghostly appearance! They were landed at "Bristol Basin" (Plainville), where they were loaded into several large wagons, and transported overland to Hartford . . . to be tried for "murder and piracy on the high seas."

Alonzo thought there were four women in the group. Actually there were four young people—a boy and three girls.

I remember seeing one . . . as she was stepping off the canal-boat, stoop down and wipe the dust off her shoes with her handkerchief.

A vivid memory for a small American boy who was not even used to seeing American blacks in Connecticut in 1839, let alone native Africans, as these captives were. And a strange memory for an African girl, accustomed to running barefoot and free in her village on the northwestern coast of Africa, to be riding on a canalboat and looking up into the faces of hundreds of people clustered on bridge after bridge above her as she worried about the dust collecting on her new shoes.

Yet just such human details as these, about this group of African blacks, were to stir the sympathy of the entire country and excite the imagination of the world. So well acquainted did American citizens become with the stories of these Africans that something happened to the life and conscience of America. The whole ugly issue of slavery was placed more sharply before the public.

For those "pirates" and "murderers" were African men and children who had been stolen from their homeland and brought to the Western world to be sold as slaves. They were among the thousands kidnapped each year by the Spanish slave traders who operated the huge slave factories along the northwestern coast of Africa.

The Spaniards purchased the blacks from other Africans who sold the captives they had taken in the constant wars that went on among the tribes, or from chieftains who sold their tribe members for "rum and guns and bolts of cloth," or from natives who owned as slaves those who had committed crimes against them.

The Spaniards bought the slaves cheap but sold them high. Because a single shipload could make a man wealthy for life, the Spanish risked the dangerous trade. Spain had outlawed slave trading in 1820, when Britain had paid her 400,000 pounds sterling to abolish it. Britain had also persuaded the nations of the West who wanted to end this traffic in human beings to establish an international police force to hunt down the illegal slavers. If a slaver was caught, he was imprisoned, his slaves were freed, and his ship was broken up and sold piecemeal.

To avoid being caught, the Spanish used long, low ships that could travel fast and had barely enough room below decks to conceal the captives. In a space no more than 3 or 4 feet high, the naked slaves were packed so tightly together that they had to sleep with one person's head against another person's thigh. In good weather they were taken on deck for

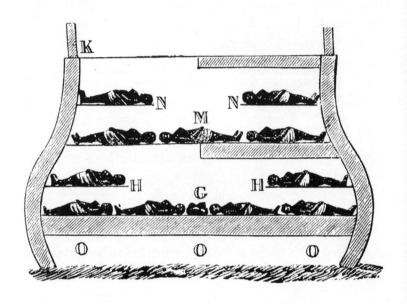

On slave ships, captives were packed
belowdecks for days at a time in a space
little more than 3 feet high.

exercise. In bad weather they were chained below, with refuse and filth collecting around them. Disease spread quickly and the sick and dying were thrown to the sharks. Those who survived the three-month passage reached Cuba only to be resold to plantation owners.

This was the usual course of events for kidnapped Africans. What was unusual about the group that Alonzo Lewis saw on the canal was that they had revolted. Sold in Havana and placed aboard the schooner *Amistad,* they were being shipped down the coast of Cuba when they rose up, killed the captain and the cook, took the ship, and ordered the Spanish navigator to take them back to Africa.

The navigator tricked them. He steered east toward Africa during the day, but at night he turned the ship back in the direction from which it had come, hoping it would be seen and recaptured by friendly Spaniards. Instead, the *Amistad* blew slowly north along the eastern coast of the United States—heading out to sea at sunrise, back toward land after dark. Off the tip of Long Island she was stopped and searched by an American ship and the Africans were taken into custody and charged with murder and piracy.

They might have been quickly condemned to death or returned to Cuba to be hanged or burned at the stake had not powerful friends come to their defense. Were the Africans murderers? Were they pirates? Or were they freemen who had a right to fight for their liberty?

The whole affair sent shivers down many an American spine, for it struck at the issue that would eventually lead the

United States into civil war. Many Americans were uneasy about slavery and yet felt that the problem was somehow not their concern. After all, the trend was away from the slave traffic, they reasoned. Most of the Western nations had passed laws against it. For over twenty years it had been illegal for citizens to bring slaves into the United States. If there were rumors that blacks were still being kidnapped and smuggled into Cuba for sale in the southern states, how could one know this for fact? And if it were so, would not the policing patrols stamp it out?

Yet any American who had looked the other way before the Africans arrived found slavery much more difficult to ignore after their stories began to appear in the newspapers. The *New York Journal of Commerce* reported on the Africans' trip from Africa to Cuba:

> On board the vessel was a large number of men, but the women and children were far the most numerous. . . . The space between decks was so small . . . they were obliged to keep a crouching posture. . . . They suffered . . . terribly. They had rice enough to eat, but had very little to drink. If they left any of the rice that was given to them uneaten, either from sickness or any other cause, they were whipped. It was a common thing for them to be forced to eat so much as to vomit. Many . . . died on the passage.

Descriptions like this one jerked the reader awake. "Forced to eat so much as to vomit." Clearly the Spaniards were trying to fatten the Africans up like cattle, so that they would bring more money in the slave market. A monstrous thing! But though slaving had been outlawed *outside* the United States, *inside* the country slaves could still be bred as cattle are bred, and sold in the market.

The thought nagged, because the Africans were so clearly not cattle. There was Ko-no-ma, the so-called "cannibal," whom the *New London Gazette* had called at first "the most horrible creature we ever saw in human shape. . . . His teeth projected at almost right angles from his mouth, while the eyes had a most savage and demoniac expression." Ko-no-ma turned out to be a gentle man from Konno, where the people forced their teeth to grow outward for beauty's sake. And there was Singbe, the "dangerous" leader of the rebellion. The public learned that he was the one who had given part of his ration of food and water to the four children on the *Amistad* during the time when they were starving. And there was the girl who got off the canalboat and stooped to wipe the dust from her shoes—a thing so universal it was remembered and written down sixty-five years later by the man who saw it.

The public began to realize that these Africans were *people.*

The *Amistad* Africans

Singbe was a farmer. He lived in the village of Mani in the Mendi country, ten days' march inland from the northwestern coast of Africa. One morning during the latter part of December 1838, he came out of the round cone-roofed hut where he lived with his wife, his three children, and his father. It was time to prepare the ground for rice planting, and he set off for his rice fields. He did not know that he would never see his family again.

Fawni was also a farmer, from the town of Bembe in another part of Mendi. He set out to work his fields one day in early January of 1839. Behind him he left his wife, his

A Mendian village as it looked in 1839.

mother and father, his sisters and brothers. Fawni, too, had left his family for all time.

Both men threaded their way through the jungle toward their fields. Near Mani, Singbe was surprised by four other Africans who slipped out of the dense undergrowth and took him prisoner. They marched him to another village, where a man called Mayagilalo used him to pay a debt. According to African tribal law, if a man could not pay his debts he either had to become his creditor's slave himself, give a member of his family as a slave, or steal someone else and sell him as a slave. So Singbe was marched to the slave factory at Lomboko on the coast of West Africa and sold to pay another man's debt.

Fawni (who was also called Funi and Foone) was seized by two Africans who sold him to a man in the town of Bembelaw, who also marched him to Lomboko and sold him to the Spanish traders.

There Singbe and Fawni waited while the slave stockade filled up with hundreds of other prisoners.

Gilabaru came. He was also a rice planter from Mendi, but he came from deep in the interior—two months' march from the coast. He was smaller than the others—only four feet eleven inches—and he wore a moustache and a beard. Singbe and Fawni could not read or write, but Gilabaru spoke several languages and the people in his country could read and write from "right to left" in Arabic.

Gilabaru had also been stolen on the trail. His uncle had bought two slaves and had given them in payment for a debt. One of the slaves had escaped and Gilabaru had been seized to take his place.

One day Ko-no-ma (also called Nazha-u-lu) stumbled into the slave pen. He had come from the very distant Konno country and therefore had less in common with any of the other prisoners. His savage appearance (which was to startle New Englanders) came not only from his tusklike teeth but also from his slit nostrils and tattooed forehead.

Pugnwawni also had filed teeth and a much-tattooed body, but his teeth had not been trained outward and so he did not look as ferocious as Ko-no-ma. He had come from a village that lay midway between the Konno country and Mendi, and he had already been a slave for two years, having been sold by his uncle to pay for a coat.

The captives came not only from Mendi and Konno, but also from Bandi, Timmani, and Bullom. Among them there were not only rice planters, but also blacksmiths like Sessi and hunters like Pie and Fuliwulu. Gbatu was the son of a nobleman; Fang, the son of a king.

Moru had been an orphan. His master had sold him to the Spanish, perhaps to pay for his "ten wives and many houses." Fuliwa, who was also called Fuli, had been captured when his village was surrounded by enemies in the night. Kimbo had been sold by his own king's son.

Kwong and Burna and Shule and Faginna had all been caught with other men's wives. In West Africa a man committing such a crime became the slave of the man he had wronged. Shule, who had been enslaved to Maya because of

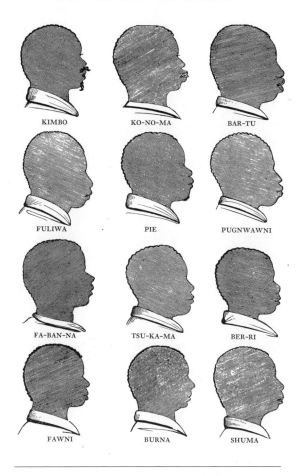

KIMBO   KO-NO-MA   BAR-TU

FULIWA   PIE   PUGNWAWNI

FA-BAN-NA   TSU-KA-MA   BER-RI

FAWNI   BURNA   SHUMA

*Profiles of some of the African captives,
taken from life and said to be "striking and
accurate likenesses."*

misconduct with Maya's wife, was walking with his master when both were set upon by Africans looking for unprotected persons to sell as slaves to the whites.

There were also some women and a few children: a boy named Ka-li who had been stolen in the street of his village and three girls—Teme, kidnapped from her home, and Kagne and Margru, both given by their fathers to men to whom they owed debts, and then sold by those men when the debts were not paid.

And so they all waited—packed together, but mainly strangers to one another, separated by differences in customs and language, speaking as many dialects as there were tribes among them.

THE UPRISING

In late March 1839, two months after Singbe was brought into Lomboko, the schooner *Teçora* came into port to trade, and several hundred slaves were herded on board. The Atlantic passage was stormy, and the Africans rolled about until parts of their bodies were rubbed raw. When the ocean grew calm, the heat increased their thirst and discomfort. They did indeed suffer terribly, as they later told reporters.

Finally, in June, they sighted land. They were put ashore and thrown into the slave pen at Havana. This time, the wait was short. After ten days a young Spaniard named José Ruiz came to buy. He selected forty-nine slaves; Singbe,

Fawni, and their companions were among them. Ruiz paid $450.00 for each of them, then he went to the office of Governor-General Espeleta and paid $10.00 apiece for a pass that gave him permission to ship the slaves to his plantation at Puerto Principe, in Cuba.

No one asked Ruiz where the slaves had come from. No one asked him if these were Cuban slaves. Yet in 1820 the Spanish Crown had made it a crime to import slaves from Africa. Only slaves who had been in Cuba since *before* 1820 could be legally shipped. But the governor-general ignored the law, signed the passes, and pocketed the money.

That night, Ruiz marched his forty-nine slaves through the streets of Havana to the harbor, where the coastal schooner *Amistad* was anchored. The Spanish word *amistad* means "friendship," but the Africans could not read Spanish. What they could understand was the whip and the gun that forced them to board the schooner.

An elderly Spanish gentleman, Pedro Montes, also bound for Puerto Principe, had arrived earlier and was settled in with his purchases—the three little girls and the boy Ka-li.

At dawn on June 28, 1839, the "long, low black schooner" topped with a headful of billowing white sail got under way briskly. Puerto Principe was only three hundred miles down the coast and Captain Ramon Ferrer expected the trip to take no more than two days. But their fast start proved deceptive, for the winds shifted. So little headway had been made by the second day that the captain realized the passage might take as long as two weeks. On board he had

La Amistad

only enough food and water for five days, so he ordered a cut in the blacks' rations, giving them only "half eat and half drink."

Cutting food and drink proved to be a foolish measure. The blacks were not chained on this trip as securely as they had been on the Atlantic passage. Their heavy neck irons were still used at night, but during the day they were chained only by the wrists and ankles and they were allowed up from the hold in groups of ten to eat and to exercise on deck. When they began to suffer from thirst, two of them who were on deck stole to the water cask and helped themselves. Members of the crew caught them at it, and Captain Ferrer had Fuli whipped. Then he was whipped again four times during the night. The next day, Kimbo, Pie, Moru, and Fawni were beaten, and their wounds were treated according to the painful custom of the time, by rubbing them with salt, gunpowder, and rum.

The floggings drove the Africans to fury. They had endured the sufferings of the Atlantic voyage and their patience was at an end. To make matters worse, Singbe, by "talking with his fingers," had asked Celestino, the mulatto cook, what was going to happen to them. Celestino made a cruel joke. He "told" them they would be killed, chopped into pieces, and salted down for meat for the Spaniards.

The Africans did not find the joke funny. None of them were cannibals and the idea of white men feasting on their flesh filled them with horror. They began to talk and plan among themselves. Though they spoke different dialects, most were Mendis, and certain words they all knew were similar. They turned to Singbe, their natural leader, who urged them to revolt. "We may as well die in trying to be free as to be killed and eaten," he said.

The slaves knew that among the cargo were boxes of the large, sharp knives used in Cuba for cutting sugarcane. These could be turned into weapons; though they had no guns, the slaves were forty-nine adults against the Spanish captain, his two crewmen, Ruiz, Montes, and the two mulatto slaves— Celestino and the cabin boy Antonio.

To get to the weapons, however, the Africans needed freedom from their chains and favorable weather conditions. When Singbe was called on deck to exercise and felt a loose nail beneath his foot, he picked it up and hid it in his armpit. Then, on the fifth night, it rained very hard. All crew hands were called on deck to manage the ship, and the sound of the downpour hid the noise of the slaves working in the hold. While the children were asleep, Singbe went to work to pry open the padlock anchoring the chain threaded through the Africans' neck irons and fastened to a ringbolt on the deck. When the padlock snapped, the men turned in a frenzy to rid one another of the smaller chains. The first men free rushed to the cargo and broke open the boxes of cane knives. The children awakened and Singbe ordered Ka-li to keep them quiet.

The rain had begun to peter out and the Africans waited silently belowdecks while the captain and the passengers settled down to sleep; Celestino lay down beside his master

Hale Woodruff portrayed the mutiny aboard the Amistad *in one of a series of murals he painted at Talladega College, Alabama, one of the higher education institutions founded by the American Missionary Association.*

on a mattress on the deck. The slaves waited until it grew very late, and then, while the clouds still covered the moon, they ripped off the grating of the hold and rushed for the deck.

Singbe found Celestino and killed him with a single blow. The captain fought back until Singbe and some of the others overpowered him; then he, too, was mortally wounded. Montes was attacked, but managed to break free, rush below, and wrap himself in a sail. The children were now on deck, screaming with fright. In the confusion the two Spanish sailors lowered a boat and slipped away.

Singbe found Montes and wanted to kill him, but the others prevented it. The Africans would need the Spaniards—especially Montes, who had once been master of a vessel—to help them sail the ship back to Africa. Antonio also was spared because he was the only one on board who could act as interpreter for the Africans and the Spaniards.

Montes and Ruiz were now lashed together while the Africans ransacked the cabin and the cargo, which included everything from glass doorknobs to Spanish shawls, from gingham umbrellas to a trunkful of gold doubloons. They broke open the casks and boxes of food, eating as they hunted, strewing food and goods about the decks—dishes and clothing and raisins and jewelry and beef and medicines and wines. They ate and drank their fill, mixing the medicines with the beef and raisins and washing it all down with wine. While the ship blew with the wind they celebrated their victory. They threw the dead overboard—including two of their fellow Africans who had been killed in the struggle along with Celestino and the captain—and they washed down the decks. They danced and shouted until some fell down drunk. Some became sick from the medicines, and two more died.

In the morning, Singbe appeared on deck dressed in a pair of white pantaloons, with a red scarf at his neck and the captain's sword fixed at his belt. He made it clear that he would be in command of the ship. He had Montes brought up from below and ordered him to steer the *Amistad* back to Sierra Leone. Montes understood the cane knives flashing above his head and he turned the ship east, straight into the rising sun. Singbe now ordered those Africans still able to walk to set the sails as Montes directed. But they knew nothing at all of sailing; the flapping canvas jerked out of their hands and the ropes danced away in the wind. The Africans soon climbed down from the rigging, leaving only the jib and the topsails to catch the wind.

The weather had begun to turn cooler. The Africans had been naked in the hold, and they began rummaging about in the cargo for odd bits of clothing and bright-colored silks and satins, to dress themselves as Singbe had done.

Thus fantastically dressed and sailing their strangely appointed ship, the Africans began the voyage that would make them famous throughout the world.

THE STRANGE VOYAGE

Each morning when the Africans awoke, the ship was sailing east toward the sunrise and home. Each night, as soon as it grew dark, Montes eased the vessel around and steered back toward Havana by the stars. When gale weather set in and the Africans lost all sense of direction, the Spaniards hoped to gain time going west; but the gale blew the ship northward, out of the channel between Cuba and Florida and up along the coast of the United States.

Back and forth she zigzagged throughout July. When the ship ran out of water, Singbe ordered Montes to put in at an island or a key to fill the empty water casks. The food problem was not so easily solved. By the end of July, Singbe had posted a heavy guard over the supplies and was portioning out food, taking least for himself and giving only the children a full measure.

The ship grew more and more sluggish, her sails rotting against the masts, her bottom heavy with barnacles and sea grass. In the August heat the blacks grew sullen and despairing. Africa seemed an endless distance away, if indeed the ship was headed for Africa. As Singbe grew more bewildered and confused he ordered Montes again and again to drop anchor. Once when they were on the high seas, Montes protested that the anchor would not catch. Singbe, determined to trap this cheating Spaniard, jumped overboard and plunged down along the anchor line. There in the open water he saw the anchor dragging free. The very act underscored his helplessness. He was commander of a ship he could not navigate; he did not know where it was now or where it was going; his passengers were slowly starving to death. Six more of the Africans had already died, either from sickness or from eating the medicines at the time of the revolt. Some lay curled on the deck like skeletons. Singbe did not know whether to risk more deaths or to put in at some island and take the chance of enslavement. The islands were not tropical; nothing about them suggested the coast of Africa. Yet he was certain the ship was near some coast, for the Africans had begun to sight other vessels.

The *Amistad* was, in fact, in New York and Long Island waters, and on August 24, on shore in Manhattan the *New*

York Times published a report that "the pilot boat *Blossom,* on Wednesday last, off the Woodlands, fell in with a Baltimore built schooner . . . having on board, apparently . . . all blacks, who requested something to eat and drink. . . . She appeared to have been a slaver, whose slaves had risen upon the captain and crew."

On shore in Norfolk, Virginia, the *Norfolk Beacon* carried an item reporting that on August 20 the captain of the schooner *Emeline* had fallen in with and boarded a schooner in an almost helpless condition. The passengers were out of water and had been forced to drink salt water for several days previously. He had found twenty-five persons on deck and a number in the hold, apparently in a state of starvation—all black men. The *Emeline* had taken the schooner in tow, but when the captain saw that the blacks meant to board his ship, he cut the towline.

Other ships reported encountering the suspicious vessel. Some boarded her and offered help, then grew afraid and cast off; others hesitated at her appearance and veered away.

The Collector of Customs in New York now dispatched a cutter to hunt down the *Amistad,* and he also sent a suggestion to the collector at Boston that he do the same. The steam frigate *Fulton* put out from New York to search. Frightened sailors up and down the coast talked among themselves. Was the "black schooner" a pirate ship waiting to attack a coastal town? Was she a slaver? Were cannibals loose on the coast? Capture her! came the cry.

None of the ships sent to hunt down the *Amistad* found her, and those that came upon her by chance steered clear and left her to pursue her aimless course alone.

Taken Captive Again!

Singbe finally dropped anchor off Culloden Point near the tip of Long Island, and on August 26 he and a group of the Africans rowed ashore to get food and water.

While some of them were loading water casks on a cart they had borrowed from a farmer and while Singbe was bargaining for food supplies, two ship captains—Henry Green and Peletiah Fordham, who were out hunting that day—saw them. They joined the bargaining group, but they offered more than the meat, bread, and gin that the Africans had collected. Captain Green took one look at the gold doubloons that Singbe carried. If Singbe could produce enough of that gold, he managed to make the African understand, he would sail the strangers back to Sierra Leone. Singbe had the trunk brought from the ship and rattled it before the captain.

But even as Singbe was bargaining to get his countrymen back to Africa, the *Amistad* was being seized by officers of a United States government vessel. From the moment Lieutenant Commander Thomas R. Gedney and his first officer, Lieutenant Richard W. Meade, standing on the deck of the surveying brig *Washington,* had seen this tattered ship with its black crew, they had realized that she might be the much-publicized "mystery ship." If she was and they captured her, they knew they might claim prize money or salvage.

That they chanced upon her when Singbe was not aboard was their good fortune, for it was Singbe who had so managed the blacks that they frightened off other ships. It was Singbe who had kept the Spaniards out of sight. Now, without Singbe on board, the blacks gave up easily and the Spaniards burst from the hold, with Ruiz crying out for United States protection and Montes falling upon the neck of Lieutenant Meade in such hysterical relief that Meade thought he was mad.

Uncertain of what was happening, Singbe and his men started back for the ship. They were quickly taken prisoner, but Singbe, like a fly in a web, kept working to escape. His efforts were later described by a reporter from the *New York Sun.*

As soon as the ropes were made fast from the *Washington* to the *Amistad,* Singbe grew frantic. He "went below, and tying some gold about his person, he leapt out of the main hatch and at one bound was over the side." He had packed too much in the money belt and sank like a stone, but managed to work himself free.

> [He] came up about 100 yards from the vessel, having been under water at least 5 minutes. The boat was instantly manned and sent in chase of him. When the boat neared him he would stop, but just as it came within reach he would dive down and come up again some yards behind her stern. He thus employed them about 40 minutes, when seeing further attempts useless, he gave himself up.

He was taken to the *Washington,* but appeared to be so uneasy and anxious that the crew returned him to the *Amistad.* There "the poor wretches clustered about him, making the most extravagant demonstrations of joy. Some laughed, some screamed, some danced, and some wept." Singbe faced them grimly. He told them he preferred death to serving the white man: "You had better be killed than live many moons in misery."

The Africans began uttering piercing yells, and Gedney ordered Singbe back to the *Washington,* where he was manacled all night to prevent his leaping overboard. The next morning he convinced Gedney by sign language that if he were returned to the *Amistad,* he would give the commander a handkerchief of gold, which he had hidden away. He was put back aboard the schooner and sent below, but Antonio

*In 1840 Nathaniel Jocelyn painted this
famous portrait of Singbe, who was released from
prison each afternoon for the sittings.*

was sent along with him to watch and to listen. Singbe quickly collected his countrymen around him, saying:

> My brothers . . . you have only one chance for death and none for liberty. I am sure you prefer death as I do. You can, by killing the white men now on board—and I will help you—make the people here kill you. It is better for you to do this, and then you will not only avert bondage yourselves, but prevent . . . unnumbered wrongs on your children.

Antonio, seeing "how the Negroes yelled and . . . leapt about and seemed . . . under some talismanic power," quickly signaled the Americans, who dragged Singbe from the hold. While his comrades moaned and cried, Singbe rode back in the cutter, moving not a muscle, his eye fixed on the schooner. On board the *Washington,* he would not rest until the crew had taken him on deck, where he stood all night staring fixedly at the *Amistad.* "He evinces no emotion," the *Sun* reported, ". . . and had he lived in the days of Greece or Rome, his name would have been handed down to posterity as one who had practiced those most sublime of all virtues—disinterested patriotism and unshrinking courage."

The *New York Sun* reporter concluded his description by expressing an admiration and respect for the rebel leader that many people would feel in the months ahead.

What Should Be
Done with the Ship and
the Crew?

The *Washington* now towed the *Amistad* across Long Island Sound and into the port of New London, Connecticut. All up and down the shore, people saw her coming and ran for the docks. They were curious for several reasons: the two Spaniards who had gone over the side the night of the uprising and who the Africans believed "could not catch land, they must have swum to the bottom of the seas" had instead reached Cuba and reported the uprising. That news had filtered into the United States and the crowd now gathered thought this vessel might be not only the famed "ghost ship," but also the mutinous one.

Only a few people were allowed to board her—port officials, medical officers, and a reporter who was so overwhelmed by the event that he forgot to ask the most important question about the *Amistad* in New London Harbor: What was she doing there in the first place? The Africans had been found in New York waters and on shore in New York State. Why, then, should a government armed vessel forcibly remove them to the state of Connecticut? Was it because Commander Gedney thought Connecticut was "soft" on slavery? Because he thought he stood a better chance of getting prize money in Connecticut? Gedney knew that the next step would be a legal investigation to decide whether the blacks should be tried for murder and piracy; to determine to whom the ship and cargo belonged; and—most important to him—to decide whether the slaves were to be judged part of the cargo. If they were, and if Gedney were awarded a portion of the cargo, he would be a wealthy man. The prize money was his first concern.

On Wednesday, August 27, Gedney sent word of the ship's capture to the United States marshal at New Haven, who informed the United States district judge. Both men came to New London.

On the morning of August 29 a court of inquiry was held onboard the *Washington*. A few reporters were present, and also artist James Sheffield, whose sketches of this day were to become famous.

The inquiry began with a complaint filed by Ruiz and Montes against Singbe and the other adult Africans who were still alive. Then Singbe was brought in to hear the charges against him, though he understood not a word. He was kept standing through the rest of the proceedings while the court considered the evidence and heard the testimony of Ruiz and Montes. Among Captain Ferrer's papers were found the two passes issued by the governor-general of Cuba. One gave permission for Ruiz to transport forty-nine slaves; the other gave Montes permission to transport the three girls. There was no pass at all for Ka-li; this strange oversight meant that Montes could not claim him in a court of law.

Ruiz and Montes told about the events of the night of the mutiny. Although they could not name the murderers of the captain and the cook, for there had been too much confusion, Antonio could, for he had been awake through it all. So the court moved to the *Amistad* and Antonio went below to pick out the two slaves who he said had committed the murder along with Singbe and a fourth man who had died on the voyage.

The judge now decided that Singbe and the others should stand trial before the next circuit court, which would meet in Hartford, Connecticut, on September 17. The three girls, Ka-li, and Antonio were also to appear and give evidence. In the meantime, all the Africans were to be taken to New Haven and held in the county jail.

Two Points of View

The *Black Schooner, or, The Pirate Slaver Amistad,* a three-act play, opened on September 2 at the Bowery Theater in New York City. It had been only eight days since the Africans had been taken into custody, and within that brief time a drama about "Zemba Cinques" (obviously Singbe) had been put together for the stage. *The Black Schooner* played to packed houses for a week and then moved on to other New York theaters—the Park, the National, and Niblo's Gardens. But no drama on the New York stage could begin to rival the one being played out in New Haven, where five thousand people were paying twelve and one-half cents apiece to file through the county jail and look at the prisoners.

Singbe had arrived first, having been sent ahead separately because he was considered dangerous. In the combination tavern-jail kept by Colonel and Mrs. Pendleton he had been locked up in the "stronghold" with the common criminals. The rest of the captives arrived on Sunday, September 1. Some marched up from the docks past the mammoth crowds, and others bounced along painfully in the wagons that had been provided for the sick.

Inside the jail the children were separated from the adults and taken to a private room in the rear of the tavern. Dr. Charles Hooker of New Haven was called in to attend the ill.

Some of the Africans were very ill indeed. Three of them had died by the middle of September. But it did not take these deaths to arouse the sympathy of New Englanders. Reporters had described the condition of the *Amistad* and her sad crew, and residents of New Haven had seen for themselves the arrival of this pitiable lot of displaced persons. The captives were not only sick, but also clearly frightened, and no one could talk with them or understand their language. Singbe huddled in jail despairing. When anyone came near him, he indicated with a gesture that he expected to have his throat cut. An interpreter was just as badly needed as the doctor had been.

It occurred to Professor Josiah Gibbs of Yale College, who was a world-famous specialist in languages, that if he could discover from what part of Africa the captives came he might be able to find an interpreter for them. He called at the county jail, but when he tried to talk with the Africans he found them speaking so many different dialects that he could not clearly identify any one language. He was quite sure, however, that most of the prisoners had come from the Mendi country and he began to hunt along the New Haven docks for an African sailor who might speak Mendi. He had no luck, but he thought of a better way to conduct his search. He returned to the jail and, holding up his index finger before the captives, said "One." He was faced with blank stares. He held up another finger. "Two," he said. Then he repeated, "One, two." Suddenly one of the Africans cried out, *"Fili! Eta, fili."* Professor Gibbs took the count to ten, going over and over the numerals until he had learned them. Then he continued his search along the local docks. Later on in September he would make a trip to New York to hunt along the waterfront there for someone who understood *"eta, fili, kiauwa, naeni, loelu . . ."*

Meanwhile, others were also organizing to help. Word of the captives' plight had quickly flashed along the underground to the New York abolitionists. The abolitionists were the most fiery group among the antislavery people. On Tuesday, September 3, these "friends of freedom" called a meeting in New York and elected a committee of three: the Reverend Joshua Leavitt, who was the editor of an antislavery newspaper; the Reverend Simeon S. Jocelyn, who for a time had been the pastor of a black church in New Haven;

and Lewis Tappan, who, along with his brother Arthur, was one of the most famous men of his day.

Both Lewis and Arthur Tappan were successful New York merchants and strong churchmen who helped develop and support colleges, churches, hospitals, asylums—nearly every missionary and reform movement of the mid-1800s. They were so violently opposed to slavery that they had made bitter enemies. In 1834, Arthur's store had been mobbed and Lewis's home had been broken into and the furniture hauled to the street and burned. By 1835, it was rumored that $100,000 had been offered as payment to anyone who would kidnap the brothers and deliver them to a slave state. The Tappans, however, quietly continued their antislavery activities. Both were to be involved in the *Amistad* case, Lewis more completely. This cause would remain one of the projects closest to his heart and his purse for the rest of his life.

The Amistad committee was organized on September 4 and 5. It sent Leavitt to New Haven to see the prisoners, while Jocelyn and Lewis Tappan issued a call for money and attended to the hiring of lawyers to defend the Africans. Then, on Friday, September 6, Lewis Tappan himself went to New Haven. He reported of his visit:

> I arrived here . . . with three men who are natives of Africa, and who were joined the next day by two others to act as interpreters. . . . On going to the jail the next morning, we found, to our great

*Lewis Tappan helped form the original
Amistad Committee and, later, the American
Missionary Association.*

disappointment, that only one of the men, J.F., was able to converse with the prisoners.

J.F. was John Ferry, "a native of Geshee or Gishe," which was farther inland than the Mendi country.

> He is able to converse a little in the Mandingo dialect, but understands better that of Gallinao, which some of the prisoners can speak. Most of the prisoners can understand him, though none of them speak his Geshee dialect.

No one could understand anyone very well. Conversation was slow and halting and unsatisfactory, but a beginning had been made. The captives knew that they had concerned friends; and they had gained a voice, feeble though it was.

But other voices were also heard on that Friday, September 6. The minister from Spain, representing Her Majesty's government in the United States, sat down and wrote a sharp letter to the United States secretary of state, John Forsyth, in Washington, D.C., demanding the return of the ship, with the slaves, to her Spanish owners. He cited the Treaty of 1795, in which Spain and the United States had agreed that if one of their ships came into the other's waters during any emergency it should be helped and then allowed to return home. Furthermore, all ships and merchandise—that is, cargo and goods—that were rescued from pirates had to be returned. In the *Amistad* case, said the Spaniards, the slaves were the "merchandise." The United States must return the slaves at once. These "assassins," said the Spanish minister, must not be allowed to go unpunished for their crimes.

"Of what crime are the prisoners guilty?" thundered the *Hartford Daily Courant,* the third voice heard on that September 6. "Is it piracy?" How could it be? The Africans did not rove the seas for the purpose of seizing other vessels. On the contrary, they had been forced aboard the *Amistad* against their will. Nor were they murderers. "The slaves . . . but took the lives of their captors to regain their own liberty. They had been recently stolen from the coast of Africa, and if they had been kidnapped by an *American* citizen, this act itself would have been piracy." By United States law, anyone who took part in slave trading was subject to the death penalty. The Spaniards were guilty under United States law, claimed the newspaper.

Articles like these, appearing in New England newspapers, were making a certain gentleman in Winsted, Connecticut, very nervous. He was United States District Attorney W. S. Holabird, who would be responsible for trying the *Amistad* case in Hartford on September 17. Holabird had been appointed to office as a Democrat and he saw that this case could cause trouble for the Democrats. It was creating sentiment against slavery, yet slaveholders from the South had helped put the Democrats in power. Holabird wrote to Secretary Forsyth on September 5 and again on September 9, asking whether the slaves could be returned to the Spaniards before the case came to trial.

*Martin Van Buren, president of the
United States from 1837 to 1841.*

Forsyth forwarded the Holabird letters and the Spanish minister's letter to the president of the United States, Martin Van Buren. On the president's desk lay still another letter, from the abolitionists' lawyers. They urged Van Buren to let the case go through the courts, rather than have it decided "in the recesses of the cabinet, where these unfriended men can have no counsel and can produce no proof."

President Van Buren was faced with a difficult situation. He had been elected to the presidency in 1836 without ever stating his position on slavery. He was coming up for reelection in 1840 and he realized that if he sent the blacks back to Cuba, the abolitionists would be angered; if he sent the blacks back to Africa, the slaveholders would be angered; if he did nothing, the Spaniards would be angered. Possibly international trade would be hurt and another set of voters would be lost to him. There was only one thing he could do: he could appear helpless because the case was already in the courts where he could not interfere.

Van Buren's secretary of state had already written Holabird to "take care that no proceeding of your circuit court . . . places the vessel, cargo, or slaves beyond the control of the Federal Executive." This procedure gave the president a loophole if he needed it, but it created great problems for Holabird.

As the case came to trial the district attorney was desperately trying to find some legal way to hold Singbe and his companions within the reach of the federal executive, while the federal executive himself was hoping he would not have to face the problem at all.

Could any drama on the Bowery stage in New York even begin to rival a plot involving an African farmer, an American president, and the courts of the United States in so strange a series of events?

PEOPLE OR PROPERTY?

On September 14, 1839, the *Amistad* captives left New Haven for Hartford by canalboat. Thousands of people had collected along the way—among them the small boy Alonzo Lewis, standing on the bridge at Plainville. But though to Alonzo's startled eyes "fifty or more Negroes" appeared to be on the boat, there were in reality only thirty-five adults along with the children, since three Africans had died in this month of September and one was too sick to make the trip.

In Hartford, as in New Haven, the captives drew enormous crowds of persons who paid their way into the prison to see them. One visitor who came was Thomas Gallaudet, founder of the first school in the United States for persons deaf and mute. He tried to work out a sign language with the Africans, for he was appalled at what lay ahead of them. These rice farmers, leopard hunters, blacksmiths, and warriors were about to face the complicated legal machinery of the United States.

Since matters relating to ships at sea were considered the concern of the *united* states, rather than of a single state, the *Amistad* case would be tried in the federal courts instead of in the state courts. Both the federal district court and the federal circuit court, meeting in the Hartford courthouse, would hear the case—the circuit court deciding on the murder and piracy issue, and the district court deciding on the property and salvage issues.

As far as the Africans were concerned, they had only one problem: to get back to Africa. Actually, the many problems they were to face in the trials that lay ahead were staggering.

The government charged Singbe and the others with murder and piracy.

Lieutenant Commander Gedney, along with Lieutenant Meade, filed suit to obtain salvage on the ship and the cargo (including the Africans) because the two officers had boarded the drifting ship and towed her to port.

Captains Green and Fordham filed claims for salvage because they had helped prevent the Africans from escaping by detaining some of them on shore.

Montes filed suit claiming part of the cargo and the three little girls as his property. Ka-li could not be claimed.

Ruiz filed suit claiming part of the cargo and the rest of the Africans, except Ka-li.

The Spanish consul filed a claim on the ship and part of the cargo in behalf of the representatives of the dead Captain Ferrer.

Merchants in Havana, who had shipped goods on the *Amistad,* filed a claim for their property, which they said the Africans had destroyed.

Finally, District Attorney Holabird asked the court to try the claims of the Spanish minister, who wanted the Africans returned as the property of the Spaniards. If the court decided the Africans should be returned, then it should issue an order for President Van Buren to send them back to Cuba. But if the Africans had been illegally brought into the United States, the court should issue an order to enable the president to return them to Africa. Either way the case went, as Holabird saw it, the captives would be within reach of the federal executive.

Some of the best legal minds in the country would be dealing with this complicated group of charges. Roger S. Baldwin, of New Haven, who would one day become the governor of Connecticut, and John Quincy Adams, a former president of the United States, would both plead for the defense. Baldwin was involved immediately; Adams entered the case at a later date.

The first decision handed down by the circuit court dealt with the question of murder and piracy. The judge ruled that the government had no right to try the captives, because "the *L'Amistad* was owned by a Spanish subject—she sailed under a Spanish flag—was commanded by a subject of the Queen of Spain," and the murder was committed by Africans on board this foreign vessel. "The laws of Spain alone could reach the act."

The answers to many of the other charges hinged on one question: Were the Africans property or were they not?

Roger Baldwin had the three girls brought into court, partly to shame the Spanish "gentlemen," as he sarcastically called them.

Were these children property? Were they to be treated as cattle, boxes, bales? The children screamed in terror because they had been separated from the others and they did not know what this roomful of white people meant to do to them. Since no one spoke their language, no one could explain.

Montes presented the passport that had been signed by the governor-general of Cuba: "I grant permission to three sound Negro women . . . belonging to Don Pedro Montes, to go to Puerto Principe by sea."

But the girls were not women; they were children. John Ferry and another African who had visited the jail swore the girls were native Africans—the youngest, seven, and the eldest, nine. In order for them to "belong to" or be the property of Montes, they would have had to be at least nineteen years old—born before 1820, when the treaty between Spain and Great Britain had taken effect. Only those Africans who had come into Cuba before 1820 or those born to Cuban slaves were legally slaves.

Were the girls the daughters of Cuban slaves? If so, they should have been able to speak Spanish or Portuguese, which were the languages of Cuba, but they knew neither.

Furthermore, one of the slaves, with the help of John Ferry, had sworn to a statement saying that he had known two of the children.

> I, Baboo, of Bandaboo in Africa . . . say that I knew Marngroo and Kenyee, two little girls now in prison at Hartford; they were born at Bandaboo, in Mandingo, and came over on the same vessel that I did to Havana.

These children had been stolen from Africa and illegally brought into Cuba. Therefore they were not the property of Montes.

Roger Baldwin had more to say about property. The claim, he said, had been made against the cargo of the ship. But the marshal had seized these *persons*. Suppose that the "cargo" were to be sold to pay salvage to Gedney or Meade? It would then be necessary to establish a slave block in Connecticut, and these children would have to be auctioned off. Would any citizen of Connecticut permit it? Did any court in Connecticut have the power to sell men, women, and children? In Connecticut, the law presumed that every man was born free.

Ralph Ingersoll, the lawyer for the Spanish, jumped up angrily. "It is idle for the gentleman to stand here and say they are *persons* and therefore not property," he said. "In a part of these states, slaves are recognized as property."

The Supreme Court had recognized slavery as lawful and slaves as property *inside* the United States. Spaniards holding slaves legally in Cuba were exactly like Americans holding slaves in any of nine southern states, Ingersoll claimed.

The judge handed down his ruling on Monday, September 23. He said that the laws of the United States clearly stated that slaves were property; the treaty between Spain and the United States clearly provided that property should be returned to the Spaniards.

But it was not clear whether the captives were or were not slaves. If the captives were slaves, the district court had the right to decide what to do with them. If they were freemen, it could release them. But until that issue was decided, the captives would stay in jail.

The district court would meet in Hartford in three and one-half weeks, on November 19, to hear arguments on the question.

An Interpreter Is Found

Reactions to the circuit court case came quickly in various cities.

In Boston, the Spanish consul wrote to the Spanish minister, who wrote an angry letter to Secretary Forsyth asking why the court had not released the ship and her cargo to the Spanish.

In Washington, President Van Buren called in his attorney general, Felix Grundy, handed him the correspondence on the case, and asked him for an official opinion.

In Quincy, Massachusetts, John Quincy Adams received a letter from one of the abolitionist lawyers, asking him about a point of law in the case. Though Adams was serving at that time as a member of the House of Representatives, the case would henceforth claim much of his attention.

In New Haven, the captives were returned to jail. This time, however, Colonel Pendleton escorted Singbe past the cells that held the common criminals and up to the second floor where he was put in with the delighted Africans. The court had decreed that the prisoners were no longer to be treated as criminals.

They had become, instead, the folk heroes of the day. Thousands of children were already carrying pictures of Singbe that had been sold in the streets, or were being taken to visit the exhibit of black wax masks that had been made from the captives' faces. Parents compared notes about this captive or that one whom they had seen in prison or at the gravesites of the three who had died. And every day, adults and children collected on the New Haven Green to watch the Africans exercising. It was an unforgettable sight to see one of them take a long, running leap over several of his companions, land on the back of his neck, and turn a somersault, or to see another who had been standing perfectly still suddenly flip into the air or begin to turn cartwheels. The captives loved to play jumping and leaping games and they outdid one another with astonishing feats, to the laughter and applause of their audience.

Now and again, the African children were taken for wagon rides, the girls in their calico dresses, with their shawls twisted high into turbans on their heads. And every afternoon, Singbe could be seen leaving prison under escort to go to the home of the painter Nathaniel Jocelyn, who was doing his portrait.

These colorful foreigners had captured the imagination of New Englanders. As rebels who had dared defy their Spanish captors, had rid themselves of their chains, and had made a strike for freedom, they deserved to be free, the public felt. From as far west as Ohio, money poured in for the *Amistad* people's cause. And along the waterfront in New York a distinguished-looking gentleman trudged, patiently stopping every black man he saw and holding up his fingers as he counted in Mendi, *"Eta, fili . . ."*

The Africans were in need of a better interpreter than John Ferry. They required someone who could speak Mendi fluently and could translate for them in court as fast as they could talk. Professor Gibbs found him. His name was James Covey and he had been born in the Mendi country, taken into slavery, and released when the British had captured the ship on which he had been imprisoned. Covey had been returned to Sierra Leone and there had chosen to study at the Church Missionary Society, where he had learned English. Now he was a seaman and an interpreter with the British navy. The captain of his ship was glad to give leave to Covey and another Mendi-speaking black to help with the *Amistad* case.

Gibbs arrived in New Haven with the seamen one crisp morning in early October, just as the leaves were turning color on New Haven Green. The captives were at breakfast when Covey entered the jail, but he walked up to the bars and began speaking Mendi in a loud voice. With a shout of joy that was never forgotten by those who heard it the captives swarmed toward him.

Now followed hours of questioning that were conducted through the interpreters. On October 7, the captives told their stories in great detail to newsmen from Boston, Hartford, New Haven, and New York. Interviewed separately, they repeated the same stories. No one listening doubted the truth of what they said.

The interview day had been carefully planned by the abolitionists. That morning, the lawyers had taken sworn statements from Singbe, Fuli, and Fawni in New Haven county court. The attorneys intended to file suit against Ruiz and Montes, charging them with falsely imprisoning and abusing the Africans who, said the lawyers, were freemen. The news conference was held that afternoon so that the American public could read of the abuse inflicted by the Spaniards on these freemen.

Ruiz and Montes were arrested in New York on October 17. They could have been freed on bail, but they chose to go to jail—"to excite sympathy & to embroil this Government with Spain," wrote Lewis Tappan to a friend.

The arrest did more than cause an uproar in Madrid and Washington. As Tappan noted further,

> The pro-slavery press, and the Southern slave-holders . . . are greatly exasperated & I doubt not it will exasperate the tyrants . . . throughout the country. But we shall try the question in our

courts & see if a man, although he is black, can-
not have justice done him here.

The Spanish minister immediately demanded that the
president free Ruiz and Montes. Van Buren replied that he
could not interfere with the courts. What was the *Amistad* case
doing in the American courts in the first place? the Spanish
minister asked. Spain had a treaty with the United States and
if the secretary of state did not have the authority to fulfill the
treaty, then, of course, it was not binding on Spain either.

That statement was strong enough to make the president
view the Spanish claims with a little more sympathy, but he
had other reasons as well. Attorney General Grundy had delivered his official opinion. He believed that the United States
was bound to honor the Treaty of 1795 and that it should
return the ship and slaves to Spain. He had only one suggestion. Since there did seem to be a chance that the Africans had
been kidnapped, they should not be turned over to Ruiz and
Montes, but to the Spanish minister in the United States, so
that they might have a chance to fight for their freedom.

The Spanish minister was told that this was the official
government opinion, which had been adopted by the president's cabinet. Just as soon as the courts had finished with
the matter, the slaves would be returned to the Spanish.

When the case against Ruiz and Montes came to court
in mid-November, Ruiz was let out on bail, but chose to go
back to jail. Montes was freed and immediately took a ship
for Cuba. He passed out of the lives of the Africans forever.

A BACK-AND-FORTH GAME

When the first snow fell on New Haven Green in November, it was a source of delight to the captives and to the Yale Divinity School students who had been spending days with the Africans, trying to teach them English. Had they ever seen snow in their native land? asked a teacher. Yes, was the reply—"Little, little, little," and then they added, "Water, water, water." This meant, their teachers decided, that "a very little snow falls, but very soon changes its form to water. This leads us to suppose their country mountainous and probably healthy."

The English lessons had grown out of the community's concern that the Africans had no way to communicate. Under the leadership of the Reverend George E. Day, the seminary students had begun their teaching by using picture cards of animals and drilling the Africans in the names and their alphabet letters. After James Covey joined the group as interpreter, the sessions in the jail gradually assumed the form of a school, with the Africans studying reading, writing, and religion as much as four or five hours a day. This indoor activity proved welcome, for that winter was the longest and coldest in years.

Six of the captives left their studies and went back to Hartford when the district court was called into session on November 19. But they shortly returned to their schooling, for the judge decided to postpone the case, because of illness and emergencies, until the next meeting of the court in New Haven on January 7.

One witness had come all the way from Cuba to testify, however, and he could not stay until January. He was Dr. Richard Robert Madden, the superintendent of liberated Africans in Havana, Cuba. The judge took Madden's testimony privately in his chambers.

Dr. Madden knew the slave trade well and he knew Cuba. Before serving in his present position, he had sat at the Mixed Court of Justice in Havana; it had tried illegal slavers and had ordered freed slaves sent back home.

Upon his arrival in the United States, Madden had gone to New Haven and talked with the prisoners. Now he stated that he knew with certainty that they were *bozales*—a word used in Cuba to refer to blacks recently brought from Africa.

He had also been shown the passes that Governor-General Espeleta had signed, in which the Africans were called *ladinos*. Madden explained that this word was used in Cuba to refer only to blacks who had been living there prior to 1820, before the treaty between Spain and England had gone into effect.

Thus, *bozales* were illegal captives and *ladinos* were legal slaves. By signing the passes, the governor-general had committed a fraud, turning the *bozales* into *ladinos* without a question being asked. In return, of course, he had pocketed the money he received for each captive.

Furthermore, Dr. Madden testified, though slave trading had been made illegal, from twenty to twenty-five thousand slaves were still being brought into Cuba each year, and the Spanish authorities "never interfere to stop this . . . trade and transfer, but connive at it."

Madden's testimony was damaging, as he intended it should be. For years he had watched the Spanish disregard the law and had been unable to stop them. Now he had a chance to strike a powerful blow against the slave trade. He went from Hartford to Washington, where he conferred with the British minister, and then on November 25 he took a ship for England where he talked with Queen Victoria about the case.

On the day he left, his testimony was published by the *New York Journal of Commerce* and by other newspapers up and down the coast. The Africans' cause had gained.

Or had it? From November 25 until the trial began on January 7, the forces for and against the return of the captives ranged themselves against one another—one making a move, another blocking it and making a countermove. Day by day the situation seesawed back and forth.

On November 26, the Spanish minister began bombarding Forsyth with a series of furious letters. He protested against the actions of the abolitionists and the charges against the governor-general of Cuba. Such charges, he warned, invited a break between the two governments. The whole *Amistad* affair offended the Spanish nation.

Something had to be done—and soon—to avoid a breach in international relations. Van Buren, as president, was pledged to protect and defend the nation, and a break with Spain would be a serious matter. During December the secretary of state held a number of conversations with the Spanish minister to assure him of official sympathy for his claims. On December 28, Forsyth told the Spaniard that he believed the Connecticut court would find itself incompetent to deal with the *Amistad* case, and that when that happened, the Spanish should be ready to take over the *Amistad* and to transport her cargo and the blacks to Cuba.

Yet there was one man in the United States whose prestige ranked higher even than the president's; he was John Quincy Adams. Adams now wrote offering his legal services to the abolitionists, and the *Hartford Courant* published his letter on December 30.

The same day, however, the Spanish minister wrote to

Forsyth, saying that he had decided the *Amistad* was too hope-lessly battered to be used to take the captives back to Cuba. He asked the United States to provide a government ship.

On January 2, 1840, the secretary of state wrote to the secretary of the navy, ordering a vessel

> to convey the Negroes of the *Amistad* to Cuba . . .
> to anchor off the port of New Haven, Connecticut
> . . . Lieutenants Gedney and Meade to be ordered
> to hold themselves in readiness to proceed in the
> same vessel. . . . These orders . . . given with spe-
> cial instructions that they are not to be communi-
> cated to any one.

It was not necessary to communicate this news to any-one. With much of the country and a good part of the world watching New Haven, the secret was out when the United States schooner *Grampus* came "through the snowy hurri-canes of the northeast" to berth in New Haven Harbor.

The abolitionists organized themselves in shifts to watch the jail and the harbor. If the government made a move, they meant to pass the captives along the underground to Canada or to spirit them away by ship to a hidden spot along the coast. There were rumors that the portrait painter Nathaniel Jocelyn had obtained a sloop, provisioned her, and slipped her into the harbor, to be held in readiness.

On January 5, the British queen ranged herself on the side of the captives. The British government wrote to the Spanish royal court calling upon Spain not only to release the captives, if they were returned to Cuba, but also to bring Montes and Ruiz to trial.

On January 6, Secretary of State Forsyth informed the Spanish minister that President Van Buren was issuing a warrant to deliver the Africans into his hands after the trial.

And on January 7, the trial itself began again in New Haven.

DECISION FOR FREEDOM

I t was perfectly clear to the faculty of the Yale Law School that their students could learn more in the courtroom, studying this case, than in the classroom. Classes were dismissed and the students went to the statehouse to hear the eight lawyers who were speaking for the various groups. The courtroom was packed. Doubtless the fact that Singbe was to testify was one of the attractions.

When the slaves had first been captured, a reporter had written of Singbe: "This Cinquez is one of those spirits that appear but seldom . . . possessing courage . . . accustomed to command." And Lewis Tappan had written at a later date,

"His natural, graceful, and energetic action, the rapidity of his utterance, and the remarkable and various expressions of his countenance excited the admiration. . . . He was pronounced . . . one born to sway . . . his fellow-men."

Singbe did just that. With dignity and thoughtfulness, he answered the lawyers' questions. Madden's testimony had been important, but so was the African leader's. At one point he got down on the floor to show the court how the captives had been forced to lie in the hold, and the court grew deathly quiet. Yet something about this assembly of people asking detailed questions and searching for exact meaning began to agitate Singbe. As the questions came thicker and faster, Singbe suddenly rose and overwhelmed the court with a passionate cry: "Give us free! Give us free!"

The court argued the case for five days and then recessed for Sunday. On Monday, January 13, 1840, Judge Judson handed down his decision, ruling first that this district court had the right to try the case.

Captains Green and Fordham, the judge said, were not entitled to salvage, but Gedney and Meade should be awarded one third the amount of the ship and the cargo.

The slaves were *not* to be part of the salvage. In Connecticut the value of a slave was not one cent.

Then the judge took up the key question: Should the Africans be delivered to the government of Spain?

These are the facts that I find proved in this case.

In Cuba there are three classes of Negroes . . .
Creoles, who were born within Spanish dominion;

Ladinos, who have been long . . . on the island . . .
so that the laws of Spain operate upon them . . .
and lastly *Bozals* . . . recently imported from
Africa.

I find these Negroes to be *Bozals.*

The law of Spain, said the judge, prohibited under
severe penalty the importation of Africans into Cuba. The
"Amistads," he said, were imported in violation of that law,
"and be it remembered, that by the same law of Spain, such
imported Negroes are declared to be free in Spain."

Why should these *bozales,* therefore, be given up under
the treaty? To have the Cubans try the question whether they
were slaves or not? Spanish law already said that they were not.

Antonio, however, was a *creole,* and should be returned
to the dead Captain Ferrer's relatives.

The judge concluded:

I shall put in form a decree of this Court that these
Africans, excepting Antonio, be delivered to the
President of the U.S. to be transported to Africa,
there to be delivered to the Agent appointed to
receive and conduct them home. To do it we have
ample authority and ample means. What American can object to this decree? No one surely, when
the case is correctly understood.

But the judge was wrong. There were many who ob-
jected and among them was the president of the United States.

STILL IMPRISONED

For a few days after the court decision the captives believed they were returning home and they made plans. They wanted one of their teachers to go with them, "to teach us, our brothers, our sisters and children." One of the divinity students asked how the Africans would treat him if he decided to go back with them. The Africans replied that they would "give him a house and abundance of food, take the best care of him and not let him be sick." But, said the student, if I grow weary on the long walk into your country, since no horses go there, what will you do with me?

For a moment the Africans were puzzled. Then Singbe

> rose from his seat—called for a blanket—tied the corners of each end together—then putting the broom handle through under the knots—placed one end upon his own shoulder, rested the other upon that of one of his companions, then thrusting his hand into the blanket and crying out, "Mr. _____ in there. Mr. _____ in there!" commenced his march.

Such plans were cruelly dashed on January 17, when the district attorney appealed the verdict of the district court as he had been ordered to do by the president. Van Buren had no intention of providing a ship to take the Africans home. The orders for the *Grampus,* after all, had read "Cuba," not "Africa."

Why had the *Grampus* been called up in the first place, asked the antislavery press, the public, and John Quincy Adams, who labeled the orders "lawless and tyrannical." On February 10, Adams put forth a resolution in the House of Representatives, requesting the president to deliver to that body copies of all the national and international correspondence relating to the case.

The material was published as House Document 185, and the public as well as the members of Congress read it. Van Buren was now accused of trying to manage the courts, of trying to affect a judge's decision, of secretly ordering up a ship. Only the latter was true, but Van Buren's enemies used all the accusations against him in the presidential election of 1840.

"Did not the President know, when he signed that order for the delivery of MEN . . . to be carried beyond seas, he was assuming a power that no president had ever assumed before?" asked John Quincy Adams when he argued the case before the Supreme Court a year later.

Roger Baldwin agreed. The federal constitution divided the government into three separate departments, each independent of the other, he said, and when the executive branch takes over what belongs to the judiciary, then "liberty ends and tyranny begins."

By the time Baldwin and Adams spoke before the Supreme Court, Van Buren had been defeated at the polls by William Henry Harrison. The *Amistad* case had helped to sharpen feeling between the North and the South, between those for slavery and against it, and it had played some part in the fortunes of a president.

The Africans suffered through that bitter winter of 1839–40, enduring cold they were not used to and disappointment as bitter as the cold. Only their classes kept them occupied, and these continued on into the summer, when they were moved outside of New Haven to Westville.

The school day began with prayers, with James Covey translating:

> O great God,
> > *O ga-wa-wa;*
> thou art good,
> > *bi-a-bi yan-din-go;*

thou hast made all things,
bi-a-bi ha-ni gbe-le ba-te-ni.

After prayers there was a half-hour sermon on the Christian faith, and then followed reading and writing. One of the teachers has left a description of the classroom:

Not infrequently in their desire to retain their teacher through the day, they attempt even to hold him, grasping his hands and clinging to his person, and individuals offer to give him their own dinner on condition of his remaining. Sometimes they may be found gathered in two or three groups, all reading and aiding each other.

Most apt of all the pupils was the eleven-year-old boy Ka-li, who wrote in a letter to John Quincy Adams:

We talk American language a little, not very good. We write every day; we write plenty letters; we read most all time; we read all Matthew and Mark and Luke and John, and plenty of little books. We love books very much.

While the Africans were attending class, the lawyers were attending court, and the abolitionists were raising more money to continue the captives' defense.

The circuit court denied the appeal of the United States government and the Supreme Court agreed to hear the case. The captives would now go before the highest court in the land with the whole executive power of the United States and Spain arrayed against them.

But they had one powerful friend who would stand at that bar with them—John Quincy Adams.

BEFORE THE
SUPREME COURT

Adams was in his seventies. He had not argued a case before the Supreme Court in thirty years, and he knew better than anyone else what lay ahead of him. He was to write in his diary:

> The world, the flesh and all the devils in hell are arrayed against any man who now in this North American Union shall dare to join the standard of Almighty God to put down the African slave-trade; and what can I, upon the verge of my seventy-fourth birthday, with a shaking hand, a darkening eye, a drowsy brain, and with my facul-

ties dropping from me one by one, as the teeth are dropping from my head—what can I do for the cause of God and man, for the progress of human emancipation, for the suppression of the African slave-trade? Yet my conscience presses me on; let me but die upon the breach.

Adams was tired, old, and uncertain. His uncertainty grew and began to verge on panic. On December 12, 1840, he wrote in his diary:

I thought it necessary to look into the case of the Amistad captives, to prepare for the argument before the Supreme Court . . . of which I dare scarcely to think.

On January 30, 1841, he wrote:

An inflammation in my left eye threatens me with complete disability to perform my final duty before the Supreme Court . . . while the . . . pressure of preparation aggravates that disability.

On February 22, the day the court sat, Adams wrote:

I walked to the Capitol with a thoroughly bewildered mind—so bewildered as to leave me nothing but fervent prayer that presence of mind may not utterly fail me at the trial I am about to go through.

*John Quincy Adams, former president
of the United States, who argued the case for the
Africans before the Supreme Court.*

And on February 23, Adams wrote:

> With increasing agitation of mind, now little
> short of agony, I rode in a hack to the Capitol.

Adams desperately wanted the Africans freed and he
was not sure he could get it done. He had gone to Westville
to meet them in November, and he was very much aware of
their wistful longing for home. He had received letters from
them, one from Ka-li, who had labored long over his words:

Dear Friend Mr. Adams:

I want to write a letter to you because you love
Mendi people, and you talk to the grand court.
We want to tell you one thing. José Ruiz say we
born in Havana, he tell lie. . . . We all born in
Mendi. . . .

We want you to ask the Court what we have
done wrong. What for Americans keep us in
prison? Some people say Mendi people crazy;
Mendi people dolt; because we no talk America
language. Merica people no talk Mendi language;
Merica people dolt?

They tell bad things about Mendi people, and
we no understand. Some men say Mendi people
very happy because they laugh and have plenty to
eat. Mr. Pendleton come, and Mendi people all
look sorry because they think about Mendi land
and friends we no see now. Mr. Pendleton say

Mendi people angry; white men afraid of Mendi people. The Mendi people no look sorry again— that why we laugh. But Mendi people feel sorry; O, we can't tell how sorry. Some people say Mendi people no got souls. Why we feel bad, we got no souls . . . ?

Dear friend Mr. Adams, you have children, you have friends, you love them, you feel very sorry if Mendi people come and carry them all to Africa. We feel bad for our friends, and our friends all feel bad for us. . . . If American people give us free we glad, if they no give us free we sorry—we sorry for Mendi people little, we sorry for American people great deal, because God punish liars. We want you to tell court that Mendi people no want to go back to Havana, we no want to be killed. Dear Friend, we want you to know how we feel. Mendi people *think, think, think.* Nobody know what we think; the teacher he know, we tell him some. Mendi people have got souls. . . . All we want is make us free.

Baldwin spoke first for the defense before the Supreme Court on February 22, 1841, and he continued on February 23. He stressed that the Africans had been born free and had been kidnapped from their homeland. They had landed in America at Culloden Point in New York State, a state that outlawed slavery. Then they had been seized by Gedney and illegally taken to Connecticut. Baldwin asked if the United

States could aid in the enslavement of men who were actually free when they first set foot on American soil.

Baldwin's second most telling point had to do with the Treaty of 1795 between Spain and the United States, which said that property should be returned to the owner as soon as the owner proved that the property was his. The Spaniards, said Baldwin, had had a year to prove their ownership and had not done so.

Adams took the floor the morning of February 24, and the moment he got to his feet his terror left him:

> With grateful heart for aid from above . . . I spoke four hours and a half with sufficient method and order to witness little flagging of attention by the Judges.

Adams dealt with the treaty as had Baldwin, but in a different way. He had been secretary of state when the treaty had been renewed in 1819:

> the whole of the negotiations with the then minister of Spain passed through my hands, and I am certain that neither of us ever entertained an idea that this word *merchandise* was to apply to human beings.

Adams had more to say. "Old Man Eloquent," as people called him, brought all his great learning to the case. He helped the court to see the *Amistad* case in terms of the past and the future. He helped it see how its decision would affect the country and the world. And in the end, his age, which had seemed to hamper him, became a blessing. He reminded the court that he was a very old man—so old that all the judges before whom he had pleaded in years past were now dead, "gone to receive the rewards . . . on high." He prayed that the members of this court might go with consciences as clear as had those before them. In effect, he reminded each man of the limits of his own life and of his ultimate accounting for it.

On March 9, 1841, the Supreme Court rendered its decision in the *Amistad* case. Adams sent word at once to Tappan:

> The captives are free!
>
> The part of the Decree of the District Court, which placed them at the disposal of the President of the United States, to be sent to Africa, is *reversed*.
>
> They are to be discharged from the Custody of the Marshall—*free*.

And then Adams added a word for Tappan alone:

> Thanks—Thanks! in the name of humanity and of justice, to YOU.
>
> J.Q. Adams.

The Africans were free at once in the United States. They could walk out of Westville prison.

FREE AT LAST!

Because the Africans had been freed from the custody of the marshal, the president had no responsibility for them. The abolitionists would have to house the former captives and raise enough money to ship them home.

Lewis Tappan and his friends wanted to do more than that. They believed that they might be able to found a chain of missions in West Africa if missionaries were sent with Singbe and his companions to start a Christian colony.

Why not keep the Africans in America a while longer? the Amistad committee asked. While the abolitionists were raising money and hunting for the right teachers to go back with them, the former captives could become better Christians.

Arrangements were made to house the Africans in Farmington, Connecticut, a key station on the Underground Railway. But before the group could be resettled the abolitionists faced another court battle. The three girls had been "taken over" by Colonel Pendleton and his wife—the Pendletons said, "as their wards"; the abolitionists said, as "servants." The girls said they wanted to stay with the Pendletons, but when the case was aired in court, it became clear that the Pendletons had frightened the children by telling them they would again be sold into slavery if they went with the others.

The court awarded the girls to Amos Townsend, a member of the New Haven committee. They would be free to return to Africa with the others when the time came.

Antonio meanwhile "walked away" from Colonel Pendleton before the government had time to return him to Cuba. The furious Spanish accused the abolitionists of passing him along the Underground Railway over the border into Canada. Quite probably, this is what happened, though there is no record to tell us.

The "Amistads" now moved to Farmington and settled into a barn turned dormitory. During the day they "cultivated . . . fifteen acres of land," raising "a large quantity of corn, potatoes, onions, beets, &c., which will be useful to them at sea." During the evenings they continued their studies, which now went uncommonly well. Wrote one reporter: "They have taken hold of learning since leaving prison . . . and have shown singular quickness in learning." A young minister, the Reverend William Raymond, who joined the group as the first of the missionaries who would go with them, wrote: "I never had scholars learn so fast. I do not attribute this however to the excellency of my teaching but to their power of acquiring knowledge." The truth was, the Africans were looking forward to going home and felt that learning would be good for them in their own country.

They also tried to help their cause by making table-cloths and napkins, unraveling the edges of the linen or cotton squares and making with their fingers net fringes, in imitation, they said, of Mendi fashion. This handiwork was sold in the churches of New England as some of the Africans toured about, raising money through the spring and summer of 1841. Singbe and Ka-li proved to be the star performers on tour. Singbe acted out with remarkable skill the uprising and the capture; Ka-li spelled "not only any word in either of the Gospels," but spelled "sentences without any mistake."

The Africans were creating an interest in missionary work, deeply affecting the people to whom they spoke and being affected themselves by what they were learning. The interest grew in the black churches as well as in the white. A group of black Christians met in the First Colored Congregational Church of Hartford two months after the Supreme Court decision, to discuss sending missionaries to Africa. On August 18, 1841, they held a convention to form the Union Missionary Society. "Forty-three names were enrolled, being chiefly people of color, including five of the *Amistad* Africans."

Five of the *Amistad* Africans were thus charter members of the Union Missionary Society, which was eventually to join with Tappan's Amistad committee.

By August, however, the traveling group was growing tired and restless and the Africans back in Farmington were plainly depressed. Two full years had passed since they had been brought into the United States. They had been lied to, tricked, cheated, and abused, and now those people they trusted most—the abolitionists—seemed determined to keep them in America.

Raymond wrote to Tappan: "I believe that should you decide to keep them another year you would lose their confidence entirely." And Tappan also received pitiful little notes from the Africans themselves, one pleading, "My friend, I will pray for you when I go to bed and when you rise in the morning and when you go to bed my friend I want you to carry us into Sierr-leone."

One of the Africans, Fawni, would never return to Sierra Leone. Sick with homesickness, he went one August afternoon to the pond where the blacks had been swimming all summer and committed suicide by drowning. At least, the Africans reached that conclusion, for Fawni was an excellent swimmer. The full despair of these black men was thus brought home in a shocking way to the abolitionists. They would now return the Africans with all possible speed.

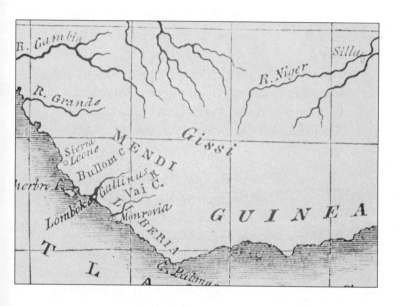

*Map of West Africa showing the Mendi
country, the island of Lomboko which housed
the slave factory, the city of Sierra Leone to which
the Africans returned, and Sherbro Island
where the American mission was founded.*

In September, Tappan wrote to the British government asking for aid:

> We have applied to the President of the United States . . . hoping that he would grant a national vessel. . . . He may think that he has not the authority, & that it will require an act of Congress. It will not do to wait for this. . . . If we send them in a Merchant vessel we fear the Spaniards will be on the look out & recapture them.

Help came from neither government, but Tappan issued calls for funds in the newspapers, and the Mendians continued their rounds performing in New England churches.

In November, the Amistad Committee chartered the barque *Gentleman.* The missionary group now assembled—an interracial one, as the committee had determined it should be. There were the two black teachers who had taught at Farmington—Mr. and Mrs. Henry Wilson—and three whites—the Reverend William Raymond and his wife and the Reverend James Steele, a widower, who had been a printer before he became a minister. They would sail with the "Amistads" to Freetown, Sierra Leone, and from there the Africans would lead the missionaries into the Mendi country.

Sad farewells were said as congregation after congregation met to give gifts to these men and children who had so touched their hearts.

In New York, on November 25, 1841, the Africans boarded the *Gentleman*. A reporter described the events of the next day:

> A steamboat towed the barque to the lower harbor. . . . As the vessel proceeded the whole company assembled in the cabin of the steamboat. . . . Mr. Lewis Tappan . . . addressed the missionaries and the Mendians. . . . At the conclusion Cinque rose and replied . . . it was a deeply affecting scene in all. . . . The whole company knelt while Deacon Townsend of New Haven offered the Lord's Prayer, the Mendians repeating each sentence after him as they have been accustomed to do.

Then the bell rang and they all gave their tearful goodbyes.

HOME TO AFRICA

The ship arrived in Sierra Leone in the middle of January 1842, and the missionaries and the "Amistads" settled in a house in Freetown.

But the homecoming was a bitter one. Singbe learned that tribal warfare between the Sherbros and the Timmanies had involved the Mendis. His village had been wiped out and the members of his family had been either killed or captured and sold into slavery. The two and one-half years he had been gone had robbed him of everything. Furthermore, the plans that had been made to locate the mission station near Singbe's village and to settle down with Singbe as headman of the region were no longer possible.

Singbe desperately wanted to go back to Mani and look for traces of his people, but he had promised Tappan to care for the missionaries and so he stayed on with them. He led a scouting party with Steele up the Boom River to look for an alternate site for the mission, but the trip was unsuccessful, and Steele caught a fever that nearly cost him his life and that sent him back to America before the year was out.

Raymond was plagued with other problems. From the moment the Africans had arrived in Freetown, they had been surrounded "by persons of every tribe of the varied popula-tion," and they found acquaintances and sometimes relatives among them. Gradually they began slipping away, to return to their own homes. Singbe was among those who eventually slipped away, though he never found any of the members of his family.

Partly to keep the remaining people together, Raymond moved them to York, twenty-five miles from Freetown, but only the four children and ten of the adults made the trip with him.

Singbe came to see Raymond at York, as did some of the others, but they stayed only a few days and then left again. The mission struggled along with great difficulty until in 1844 a strong and successful station was established at Kaw Mendi on Sherbro Island.

Over the years, the missionaries sent home news of the former captives. Some came back to the mission for periods of time and then left again; some settled near the station; some were recaptured in war, and sold again into slavery.

Only the children remained at the mission for any length of time.

Margru was eventually sent back to the United States, where she attended Oberlin College. She returned to Africa to become the principal of the mission school. Teme fell in love with John Levere, "a Moco creole" who was employed at the mission to keep accounts and assist in the school. Raymond wrote to Margru at Oberlin, "Myself, I am inclined to think it will be a good match." Ka-li married and remained for a time in the employ of the mission, though he was severely handicapped with a disease that left him crippled with badly swollen legs. Kagne died of fever at the mission in 1847, just two weeks after Raymond was buried—news which brought much grief to Margru while she was studying in the States. But before he died, Raymond had redeemed Kagne's brother from slavery, buying his freedom as he had bought freedom for twenty other Africans.

And what happened to Singbe? There are many different stories. One has it that after he left the mission, life did not go well and he returned to serve as interpreter until he died. Another says that he became a prominent and powerful chieftain among his own people; a third says that he eventually became a slave trader himself; and a fourth says that he went to the West Indies.

It is hard to tell which of the stories is true. Some of the letters from the missionaries have disappeared, as have some of the other important documents, so that a complete record no longer exists. Among the letters that are still available is

Margru was sent back to the United States to attend Oberlin College. She returned to Africa and became principal of a missionary school.

one from William Raymond, dated 1845, which says that *"Cinque* has emigrated to Jamaica." And there is a printed copy of a letter dated 1847, which says, "Cinque (or Joseph Sin-gbe, which is his proper name) is in the West Indies."

But if Singbe did go to the West Indies, he returned to Africa to live, for in 1879, when he was an old man, he came back to the mission and announced that he had come to die. He was buried in the little cemetery behind the mission. The Christian service was conducted by the Reverend Albert P. Miller, a young black missionary who had graduated from Fisk University in the United States only the year before.

That this Fisk University graduate should have conducted the funeral for the leader of the *Amistad* group was a strange coincidence indeed, for Singbe in a certain sense had been responsible for the founding of Fisk. He had led the revolt that had stirred the antislavery people to form a committee for the Africans' defense. That committee had stayed together to support the Mendi missions and then had enlarged to become the American Missionary Association. After the Civil War this association moved into the South to educate newly freed slaves. It established over five hundred black schools and colleges, among them Hampton, Howard, Dillard, Tougaloo, Talladega, and Fisk.

The story takes still another turn. Twenty-five years after Singbe died, the Reverend Albert Miller, who had long since returned to America and was serving a church in Grand Rapids, Michigan, received a letter from a fellow pastor, the Reverend Alonzo Lewis. Alonzo wanted to know what had happened to the Africans he had seen from the Plainville Bridge on the canal all those years before. Miller answered:

> I was in Africa at the Mendi Mission . . . in '78–'79
> . . . and buried Joseph Cinques, the last survivor
> of that noble band. . . . He had relapsed into
> Paganism, but lived in the Mission vicinity. Most of
> the others remained "steadfast in the faith." Some
> of their children and grandchildren were in the
> Mission when I was there, and one . . . returned
> with me to the United States and was graduated at
> the Fisk University in '91.

Only half a century had passed between the time the Africans had drifted into New York waters and one of their grandsons returned to enroll at Fisk. The black schooner had sailed out of Havana Harbor and straight into history.